RELIGIONS OF HUMANITY

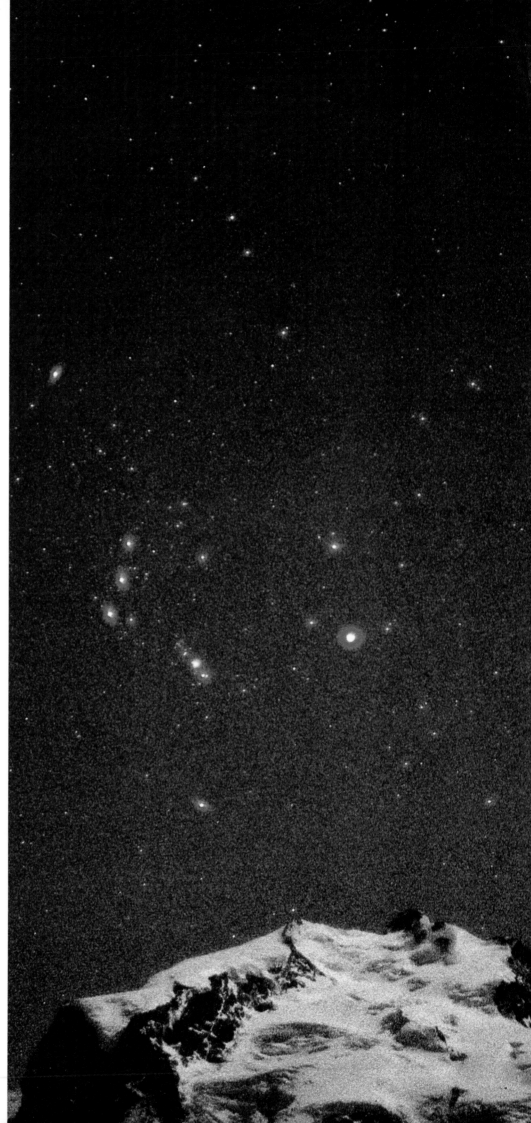

Chelsea House Publishers
1974 Sproul Road, Suite 400
Broomall, PA 19008

The Chelsea House
world wide web address is
www.chelseahouse.com

English-language edition
© 2002 by Chelsea House
Publishers, a subsidiary
of Haights Cross
Communications

First Printing

1 3 5 7 9 6 4 2

Library of Congress Cataloging-in-
Publication Data Applied For:
ISBN: 0-7910-6622-3

© 2001 by
Editoriale Jaca Book spa, Milan
Originally published by
Editoriale Jaca Book, Milan, Italy

Design
Jaca Book

Original French text by
Julien Ries

A starry night and the Swiss side of Monte Rosa in the European Alps. The vision of the celestial vault has always fascinated human beings everywhere. The changing colors, the atmospheric elements, the alternating of day and night, the appearance and disappearance of the sun, the moon and the stars, have led to man's interest, awe and reverential fear of the celestial vault. Man has experienced the sky as a natural phenomenon and as a superior reality at once. This reality is gifted with a mysterious otherness, the bringer of religious concepts. Starting from such an experience, man has composed stories about the origins of the world, celebrated ceremonies, constructed monuments, attempting to express the inexpressible, to research a connection among things, to give a sense of unity to the world notwithstanding divergent tendencies. The mountain plays then an important role in the sacred geography of religions as a tie between heaven and earth since it offers nearness to the sky and an ample perspective of the earth.

JULIEN RIES

MAN AND THE SENSE OF
MYSTERY

In Ipolera, Australia, near Alice Springs, an Aboriginal artist paints according to ancient traditional techniques. For the native peoples of Australia sacred time, in which ancestors and heroes shaped the world and the living beings, is made accessible through art. Art thus allows contact with the most profound dimension of reality.

CHELSEA HOUSE PUBLISHERS
PHILADELPHIA

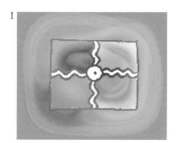

CONTENTS

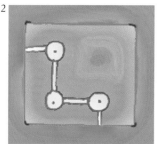

INTRODUCTION

In a world like ours, so full of signs that indicate obligatory direction (advertising, political, commercial signs, electronic routes, roads, public order signs, prohibition, danger, permission signs, etc...) there is less of a habit on the part of man to recognize *symbols*, concrete signs which refer to a more profound reality, that form a bridge with the origin and the meaning of life. Man is a symbolic being. Man needs symbols because he needs to give meaning to the cosmos, nature, his own life, and to the life of his people.

The recent discoveries, of the last forty years, on the origin of man (*Homo habilis*) and all the archeological discoveries on prehistoric art (*Homo sapiens*) show us man as a *symbolic* and *religious* man. Man must search to make a bridge with the mystery of infinity, of his origin, and of his destiny. Thus the sky, the mountain, the water, and others become the first symbols of humanity.

But man has never ceased being a symbolic and religious being: the history of all civilizations demonstrates this. In this story there are particularly important factors, with a permanent value of reference for all cultures, like the word and the link with an origin.

In this sense the cultures of Africa and Australia provoke today's reality not to loose that symbolic link which too often the faithful of the so-called great religions live formally or are led to distort in the fundamentalisms.

This volume completes the edition of twelve volumes on religions of humanity. On one hand we want to go again through the first, long steps of humanity, and on the other we want to reaffirm that the need of symbols and the religious quest are a need of today's man, as in the origin. All men are called to a research of a meaning, be it they profess a religion or be it they belong to a confession.

1. 2. 3. The art of the Australian Aborigines always includes a spiritual dimension traceable to a map, whose profound sense is not topographic but an expression of the fact that landscape and territory are traces of the incursion on earth of supernatural beings who, rock by rock, spring by spring, clearing by clearing, created a system of signs that refers to a sacred drama of the time of the origins, or Dreamtime. Man must then make himself responsible for the integration into and the preservation of this system.
The drawings (facing page) are graphic elaborations of artistic motifs from the central Australian desert. Lines and circles are connected in differing combinations and express the path and the points of rest, the journey and the stopping places of a people who had always tested itself with long distances and with the specificity of single locations. The paths of man also give voice to the paths of supernatural beings and the significant places are the locations relevant to sacred ancestors.

4. 5. Against a setting of eucalyptus, of which there are many varieties in Australia, an Aborigine is using a didjeridoo, or drone pipe, a sound-amplifying instrument made from a eucalyptus branch that has been hollowed out by termites. The empty tube is played by emitting breath and vibrating lips, producing whistles and whispers or powerful sounds. In this fashion songs and tribal formulas are recited. It is an example of how man discovers within his environment a spiritual use for objects that— by modifying reality, in this case sound—can transcend things to a different and mysterious level.
6. In Mesopotamia during the 3rd millennium B.C. the use of small praying statues became widespread. They are a variation of the universally used image of the worshipper or the offerer leaning toward the god he wants to address. Here we see the graphically modified statue of a praying prince.

1
EMERGENCE OF MAN, THE CREATOR OF CULTURE

From 1959, the scientific expeditions in Tanzania, Kenya, Rift Valley of Ethiopia, Hadar, and South Africa, brought to light a prodigious documentation of cranial and skeletal remains, often associated with choppers, hunting weapons, hammers, and other tools. To this first rediscovered culture the name of Olduvai Culture, a site in Tanzania, was given, and its creator was called *Homo habilis*. He differentiated himself from the Australopithecs, among whom he already lived about 2,500,000 years ago, because of his cranial capacity (760 cm³), spinal column, and bipedalism.

Homo habilis has shown himself capable to create. His right hand, grasping a stone with a precision grip, chopped another stone in order to make a tool of it: thus he could elaborate a project and organize his work. He chose materials, taking into account their solidity, resistance, and color: thus he had an aesthetic awareness. He chopped the stones on two opposite sides: thus he had the notion of symmetry. These are significant clues that he had an imagination and a symbolic awareness. Since the moment he started to create, man never stopped. He knew that he knew. He could evaluate with awareness. In the history of phylogenesis, we are in the presence of a qualitative change because the tool kit marks the birth of culture, sign and trace of man amongst nature. It is also the proof of the existence of a symbolic function, a distinctive element of the human species. From this symbolic function we will be able to detect the birth of the *homo religiosus*.

How did the first men live? Camp remains were found by the water. These fruit gatherers and big game hunters probably never left the African territories on which they lived from 2,500,000 to 1,600,000 years ago. Then they disappeared.

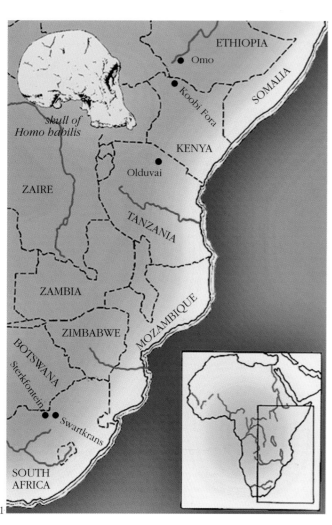

1. Map of the main sites in which fossil records of Homo habilis were found. 2. Melka Kunturé, in the heart of Ethiopia, near the Awash River, was a place frequented by prehistoric peoples in different epochs. They would camp near the water, along rocky and sandy banks. The locations occupied by Homo habilis (where choppers were found) were divided in different areas used for various activities.

3. A reconstruction of how Homo habilis could have looked.
4. The drawing shows how the area of Olduvai Gorge, in Tanzania, could look when it was inhabited by the first men, who left fossil traces of their presence.

6. *The stone is placed on an anvil and struck at an angle, in order to sharpen its edges. Within a short span of time, a new tool will be placed between the stone and the striker to obtain higher precision.*
7. *The stone shown here is chopped on two sides: after having cut one side, the operation is repeated on the other side along the edge, in order to sharpen it further.*
8. *In some sites, circles of stone associated with bones and tools have been found. Homo habilis organized his living—and perhaps even working—space.*

Through the invention of culture, *Homo habilis* gave proof of his intelligence. To the hominization is linked the humanization: awakening of thought and symbolic awareness. Language would follow, because the manufacturing techniques needed teaching.

5. *The excavations suggested that Homo habilis made stone tools in a systematic and progressive way; this is the result of a project aimed to find new solutions. The drawing shows an initial phase of this technological progress: the ability to remove a flake from a core stone with the help of another stone, in order to use both the flake and the core. The ability to make tools for varied uses after having conceived them, and the use of tools to fabricate other tools, is an evidence of a creative mind.*

2
CONQUEROR OF SPACE AND WATCHER OF THE SKY

Homo erectus, "upright man," is the name given in the 19th century to that link of the human species which made its appearance in Eastern Africa, to the east of Lake Turkana in Kenya, about 1.5 million years ago. Yet, *Homo erectus* had first been discovered in Java in 1891, before *Homo habilis* was found in 1959. From Africa he spread to Java, China, and Southern Europe. He disappeared about 150,000 years ago. His cranial capacity increased from 800 to 1,250 cm^3. His face was large and massive. He was a robust man.

This conqueror of the spaces left numerous traces of his settlements: open-air camps, stone walled areas, and remains of huts with interior spaces designed for manufacturing tools, butchering game, and the resting of the family. The organization was linked to an economy of hunter-gatherers.

The tool prolongs the hand and the mind. The bifacial chopping increases in number: it is the birth of the Acheulian with its symmetry, and it is the first step into art because, together with the bifaces, a more refined industry of flake tools, thinner and sharper, is recorded. Full-fledged lithic industry workshops have been discovered (in Terra Amata, near Nice). A first form of social structure was born.

Homo erectus invented fire and used it in fire hearths. The discoveries of Terra Amata, and those of Zhoukoudian, near Peking, bring us back to 500,000 years ago. Fire is the crucial fact of the Acheulian civilization because it is more of a mental progress than a technical one. The use of fire took place in fire hearths within caves and shelters where men lived. This means not only a drastic advance in feeding habits, due to cooking, but also the gathering of the family and of the social group: it is the creation of the human space, since the remains that have been discovered imply a maintained fire. It is easy to think about the symbolism of the fire, the relation of the domestic fire with the celestial fire, and the first fire rituals.

The conquest of spaces made by *Homo erectus* involves his perception of distant horizons and his outlook toward the sky. The latter appears as the roof of the earth, upon which it leans. In many later cosmologies the earth's disc is surrounded by mountain chains, which are columns that carry the celestial dome. The colors of the sky, the sunrise and sunset, the rainbow, the movements of the moon and stars, and the succession of the day and night must have impressed *Homo erectus*. Mircea Eliade has shown that the simple contemplation of the sky caused a true experience of the sacred to arise in the conscience of the archaic man. Here are the roots of human religiousness.

1. At first, man probably tried to cautiously control spontaneous fires, then he was able to dominate them, and eventually to produce them at will using diverse techniques: striking stones against each other, rubbing, or friction. Fire, the source of heat and light, a means of transforming certain materials and a defense against predators, became a companion to humankind.

1

2

2. Reconstructed head of Homo erectus. The skull which provided the model was found in a cave at Tautavel in the French Pyrenees mountains.
3. 4. 5. In the background a starry sky, surely the object of prehistoric man's wonder. Under Tautavel Man's skull we see the map of the diffusion of Homo erectus through Africa, Europe and Asia (in purple).

6. *Italian biface chopped on both sides used for skinning or scraping. Its shape suggests more than pure functionality. Likewise, in the English biface on the right, a fossilized shell has been kept as decoration.*

11

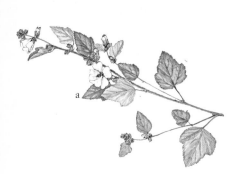
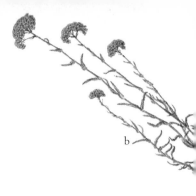

3
HOMO SAPIENS
AND HIS AWARENESS
OF THE AFTERLIFE

Starting about 150,000 years ago, *Homo sapiens* began to supplant *Homo erectus. Homo sapiens'* distinguishing feature was a voluminous brain: 1,400 cm³. In the Neanderthal Man, a sub-species of *Homo sapiens* who populated Europe from 80,000 to 35,000 years ago, the cranial capacity measured up to 1,700 cm³. The Middle Paleolithic man developed a tool industry called Mousterian: points and bifaces, scrapers, blades, burins, and bone tools. This industry represents a true complex of manufacturing techniques that required teaching, and thus language. It lasted 50,000 years.

Homo sapiens became aware of death and some form of afterlife. The first burials were discovered in Skhul and Qafzeh in Palestine, and date back 90,000 years ago. The burials of the Neanderthal Man are countless: only in France they were found at La Chapelle-aux-Saints, La Ferrassie, Combe Grenal, Le Moustier, and elsewhere. At La Ferrassie, a three year-old child had been placed in a burial covered by a slab, a sign of emotional relationship of the living with the deceased. In several burials (La Chapelle-aux-Saints, Régourdou), the excavations have unearthed remains of food; elsewhere there were traces of offerings or artifacts, such as scrapers or well-sharpened points at La Ferrassie. In burial number VI, Shanidar, Iraq, a skeleton was placed in the center of a circle of boulders: abundant pollens, dating back 50,000 years ago, covered a body placed on a bedding of Ephedra branches, garnished with yellow and blue flowers (G. Camps, *La Préhistoire*, Paris, 1982, pg. 384). We have evidence for a belief in afterlife.

In the Upper Paleolithic, from 34,000 years ago, the Cro-Magnon Man stated such belief even more clearly. In Grimaldi, Italy, and at Predmosti and Pavlov in Moravia, stone slabs protected the head of the deceased. Finery objects made their appearance, especially shells and teeth. The use of red ochre

is a significant element of which Qafzeh and Grimaldi are very eloquent examples. The treatment of yellow ochre, which becomes red under the flame, and its funerary use, are clues of a precise intention of the living: a symbol of blood and thus of life, the red ochre suggests the belief in an afterlife.

Toward the end of the Upper Paleolithic, the burial rites multiply: manipulation of the bones, cleaned of their flesh; skulls placed on flat stones and adorned with shells, as in the cave of Le Placard; and skulls with shells set in their orbits (Le Mas d'Azil). The living gave the deceased "eternal eyes."

The repetition and the diffusion of such funeral practices, which lasted more than 80,000 years in Europe, Asia, and Africa, show that *Homo sapiens* believed in a survival after death and shaped his behavior according to this belief. He was a *homo religiosus*.

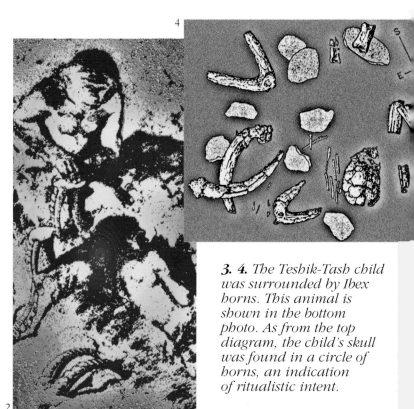

3. 4. The Teshik-Tash child was surrounded by Ibex horns. This animal is shown in the bottom photo. As from the top diagram, the child's skull was found in a circle of horns, an indication of ritualistic intent.

1. Inside a cave in Régourdou, France, the burials of a man and a bear were found in the same location. The man was placed in a hole, lying on a bed of stones and covered by a pile of rocks and sand (orange). The skeleton of the bear, possibly a cult object, was placed in a large hole nearby (black). Man's creative dedication to these burials is a sign of thought and reflection on life and death.
2. A graphic elaboration of a painting by Burian: the burial of a Neanderthal child in Teshik-Tash, Uzbekistan.

5. *The illustration recreates a Neanderthal funeral. Since pollen has often been found at burial sites, it is possible to conceive the ceremonial use of flowers, maybe tied to their medicinal use. Flowers might be a symbol of survival, or they might identify the deceased man as a healer.*

In the drawings above are some of the flowers whose pollen was found in high concentrations inside burial caves, like the one in Shanidar, Iraq:
a) *hollyhock,* ***b)*** *alpine yarrow,* ***c)*** *Jacobean lily,*
d) *muscari, and* ***e)*** *cornflower.*

MAN IN SEARCH OF THE MEANING OF THE UNIVERSE

After the first *Sapiens* the *Sapiens sapiens*, our distant ancestor, followed. He is that man of the Upper Paleolithic (40,000-10,000 years ago) we have just spoken about regarding after-life, establishing that he was a *homo religiosus*. We have seen that from his origins, man has always had a symbolic con-science capable of stimulating his creative function and per-ceiving the mysteries of the cosmos. *Homo sapiens sapiens* reached a new stage of humanization characterized by a har-mony between the tool, the hand, the brain, the intellectual awareness, and the imagination. Also, the result of his activity is the marvelous world heritage of parietal rock art, painted and engraved, and furniture art that he created along 30,000 years. This art is the only source at our disposal for the knowl-edge of his thought.

Going by the large number of injured animals represented in the cave walls, Henri Breuil has highlighted a group of magic-religious rites that are inseparable from big game hunt-ing, as is the case among today's Aboriginal tribes. On the oth-er hand, J. Clottes and D. Lewis-Williams resume the shaman-ism hypothesis, expressed in the past. They think that the cre-ation of cave paintings would be the work of shamans, initiat-ed people under the influence of drugs, who, during trances,

1. The entrance to the Mornova cave in the Bulgarian mountains. According to remains, this cave was once inhabited by the Paleolithic man. In most cultures and nearly all periods, the caves evoked a tighter contact with the earth's core, both as a safe haven, and as a sign of the significant interruption of the homogeneity of space. Often caves were sacred places used for rites of passage into adulthood and for healing. Painted walls, traces of color on the ground, and objects found inside have caused many a discussion among scholars of prehistory, but the ritual use of paleolithic caves is surely a part of an articulated world vision.
2. Prehistoric artists on scaffolds painting the walls of a cavern. The masked individuals suggest an upcoming ritual.

would have transmitted their messages stemming from visions brought back from another world.

A. Leroi-Gourhan has studied the society, the animal figures and their associations, the spatial organization of the sites, and the caves used as sanctuaries. According to him, the paintings constitute mythograms, which is to say assemblies and compo-sitions that would take meaning only when animated by the speech of the teacher initiating the young of the clan. These would then be the origins of the great myths, which are later found in the first texts, after the invention of writing.

Trying to include all the available data about cave, rock, and furniture art of the Upper Paleolithic in his analysis, E. Anati postulates "the principles, the basic concepts, the essential

4. A realistic and expressive moving lion carved in ivory, found in a paleolithic encampment in the Czech Republic. Small terra cotta and ivory statues of men and animals, as well as personal ornaments like pendants, rings and diadems were found here.

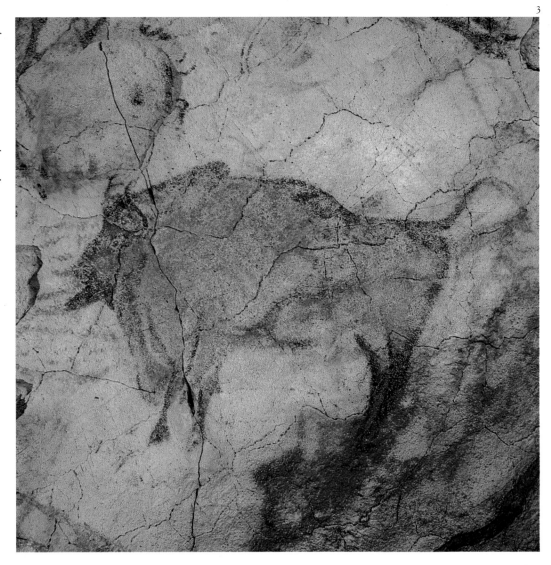

3. *A painting in the Cave of Altamira, Spain. Picasso commented on these works, which are considered the most beautiful paintings of prehistory, saying: "None of us is able to paint this way." Here we see the powerful figure of a large polychrome bison. Animals are a common denominator in Altamira, as they are in other painted caves of the time. Their strength and grace display a vital energy that, though not accessible for our classification, calls to us with a genius and mastery reaching the universal dimension of art. The painter of Altamira, who took a long time to complete such a vast complex of paintings, was surely sustained both spiritually and physically by his social group, who must have recognized his gift, a capability to give life to something they considered so essential through his art.*

canons" of an original archetypical religion whose heritage will be kept. This means that he discovers the archetype of the *homo religiosus* between the lines of paleolithic art.

These interpretations of the available documents and of the meticulous, diverse researches suggest that the Paleolithic man was in search of the meaning of the universe. By means of a symbolic and mythical language he tried to situate himself in the cosmos. He looked for the meaning of life and believed in the existence of a life beyond death. His drawings, his engravings, and his paintings are found on open air rock shelters and underground, in caves transformed into sanctuaries. Such caves still bear the footprints of young people, probably a trace of initiation sessions. The world heritage of his recovered artistic achievements is the evidence for his rich experience of the sacred.

4

5
THE SETTLED MAN BECOMES AWARE OF THE DIVINE

Toward 12,000 B.C. a phenomenon which would be crucial from then on began: man left natural shelters and settled in housing agglomerations, built by a population which exploited the surrounding environment. The first villages were created by gatherers, hunters, and fishermen. With this civilization, called Natufian (from Wadi en Natuf, in Palestine), appeared the first cemeteries, whose graves have preserved a wealth of shells and bone ornaments together with the skeletons. These are signs of the belief in an afterlife and in a "community" of the deceased.

Toward 10,000 B.C. started the Khiamian culture (from Khiam, in Palestine), identified by its arrowheads, its houses, built in bricks linked with mortar, and its female representations together with the auroch skulls embedded in clay seats inside the homes. The first female figurines were found by Cauvin at Mureybet on the Euphrates. From 9,000 B.C. the so-called "revolution" of symbols became more marked: the woman and the bull became symbols of the divine. Toward 8,300 B.C the birth of agriculture gave way to the domestication of animals and to new technologies. It is the beginning of the Neolithic Religion.

Occupied after 7,000 B.C., the Anatolian city of Çatal Hüyük, not yet completely excavated, has displayed many shrine-houses, painted frescos, high reliefs, and female statuettes. One of the frescos represents a gigantic bull surrounded by a group of tiny men in praying position, with their arms and hands raised toward the animal. These praying gestures were also found in the 5th millennium B.C. rocks of Valcamonica in Italy, and elsewhere in the Neolithic rock art. "The sacred is no longer perceived on the level of man but above him" (Cauvin). Man shows his belief in a supreme deity to which he turns.

The goddess, first human shaped deity, was widespread in the Near East. Between 6,500 and 3,500 B.C., she invaded Central Europe: Marija Gimbutas has collected 30,000 figurines from 3,000 sites in Greece and the Balkans. The masks, the symbols, and the ideograms, are the proof of the existence of rituals, therefore of a real worship.

A new cultural and religious stage in the growth of humanity, the Neolithic left us a substantial funerary documentation: ceramics and offering vases in tombs, a "house of the dead" with its red earth in Byblos, skull decorations, body embellishments, revived faces, new eyes obtained from shells set in the orbits, red ochre, personal belongings in the tombs, and the dead bodies associated to the worship of the goddess in Malta.

The great agricultural myths have their roots in the Neolithic compost: rhythm of the seasons, growth of the vegetation, birth of the cosmos, and cosmogonic myths relating to the origin of the sun and stars. The sanctuaries of the Near East, the temples of Malta, and the sacred houses of Lepenski-Vir near the Danube, confirm the practice of Neolithic worship that is at the origin of the religions of the Near East and the Mediterranean world.

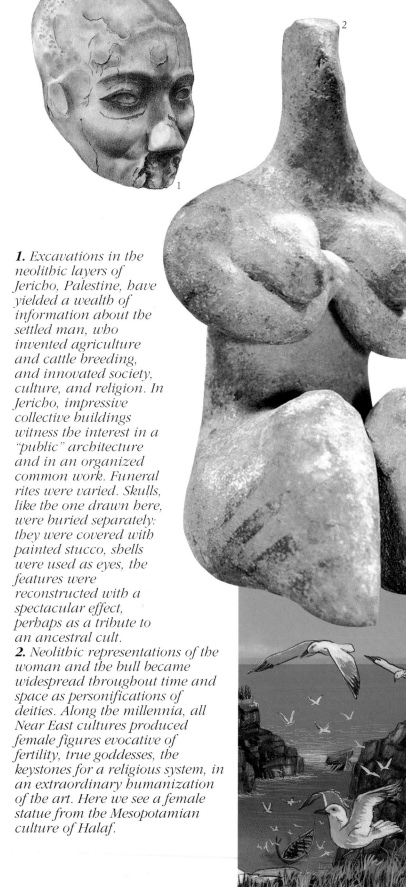

1. Excavations in the neolithic layers of Jericho, Palestine, have yielded a wealth of information about the settled man, who invented agriculture and cattle breeding, and innovated society, culture, and religion. In Jericho, impressive collective buildings witness the interest in a "public" architecture and in an organized common work. Funeral rites were varied. Skulls, like the one drawn here, were buried separately: they were covered with painted stucco, shells were used as eyes, the features were reconstructed with a spectacular effect, perhaps as a tribute to an ancestral cult.
2. Neolithic representations of the woman and the bull became widespread throughout time and space as personifications of deities. Along the millennia, all Near East cultures produced female figures evocative of fertility, true goddesses, the keystones for a religious system, in an extraordinary humanization of the art. Here we see a female statue from the Mesopotamian culture of Halaf.

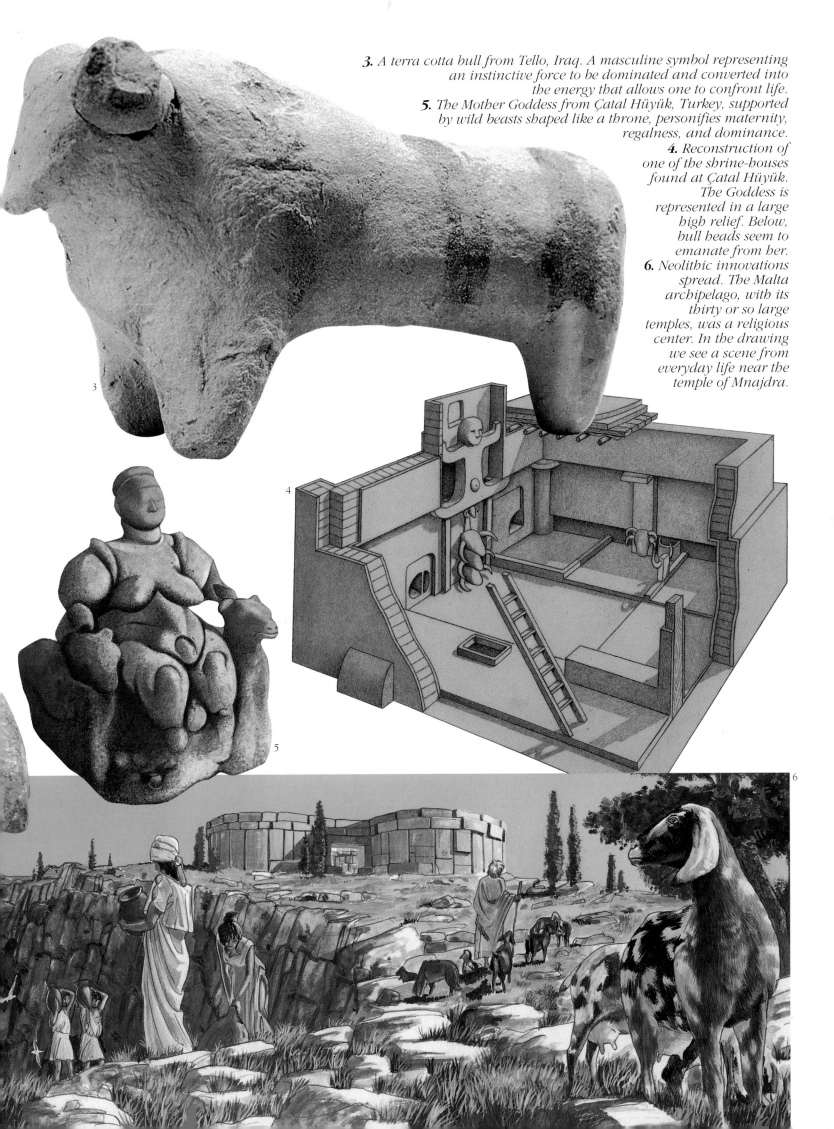

3. *A terra cotta bull from Tello, Iraq. A masculine symbol representing an instinctive force to be dominated and converted into the energy that allows one to confront life.*

5. *The Mother Goddess from Çatal Hüyük, Turkey, supported by wild beasts shaped like a throne, personifies maternity, regalness, and dominance.*

4. *Reconstruction of one of the shrine-houses found at Çatal Hüyük. The Goddess is represented in a large high relief. Below, bull heads seem to emanate from her.*

6. *Neolithic innovations spread. The Malta archipelago, with its thirty or so large temples, was a religious center. In the drawing we see a scene from everyday life near the temple of Mnajdra.*

THE RELIGIOUS MAN AND THE ORIGINS OF THE GREAT ORIENTAL CIVILIZATIONS

Toward 3,300 B.C., the Sumerians of Lower Mesopotamia perfected cuneiform writing, a brilliant invention which was at the origin of a true cultural and religious explosion known to us through half a million documents. Toward 9,000 B.C. at Mureybet on the Euphrates, man created the first symbols of the divine: the goddess and the bull. The Sumerian religious man represented his gods and goddesses in human forms, wearing a tiara with horns, a religious symbol of the bull that meant strength and transcendence. The sign of the star placed in front of the ideograms confirmed their heavenly nature. The main characteristic of the deity was light and splendor, and sometimes a halo around god's head to underline his irradiating strength. Moreover, clothes sparkled and shined inside temples and sanctuaries. The rite of the crowning of the divine statues bestowed power and majesty upon them. The epic texts show that the Mesopotamian *homo religiosus* gave the sacred its true dimension.

A substantial documentation supplied by the thousands of clay tablets passes on the myths of the creation of cosmos and man. Upon the latter, who was their servant, the gods and goddesses imposed the decree (*me*) of a heavy destiny, hence the multiplicity of the divinatory techniques necessary to know the divine will. The supreme god Anu held the primordial kingship, part of which was delegated to his earthly vicar,

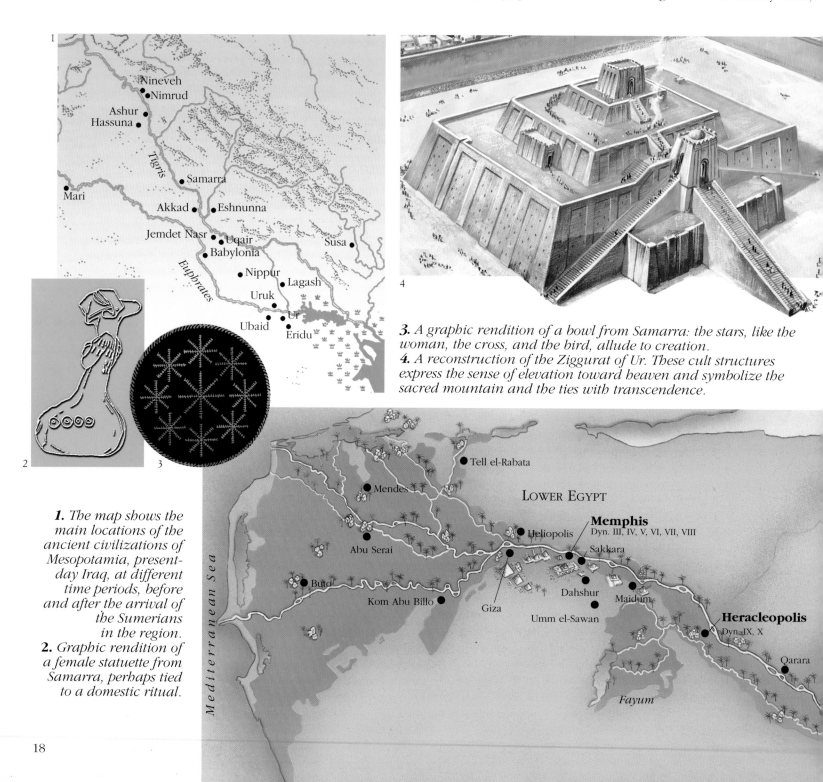

3. A graphic rendition of a bowl from Samarra: the stars, like the woman, the cross, and the bird, allude to creation.
4. A reconstruction of the Ziggurat of Ur. These cult structures express the sense of elevation toward heaven and symbolize the sacred mountain and the ties with transcendence.

1. The map shows the main locations of the ancient civilizations of Mesopotamia, present-day Iraq, at different time periods, before and after the arrival of the Sumerians in the region.
2. Graphic rendition of a female statuette from Samarra, perhaps tied to a domestic ritual.

the king. The latter was in charge of leading the human flock, promoting divine worship in the temples, and organizing feasts in honor of the gods. A priestly caste, as well as the first rituals and Eucologs, were born: the *homo religiosus* organized collective prayer, public worship, feasts, and solemn celebrations, presided over by the royal priesthood.

The inhabitants of the Valley of the Nile followed the Sumerians' footsteps. Amazed by nature, by the daily sunrise, by the annual regular and beneficial rise in the water of the Nile, and by the floods which fertilized the soil, they tried to explain such a mystery. Since the beginning of the 3rd millennium B.C., the priests of Heliopolis thought of a creator solar god, Atum-Re; those from Hermopolis imagined the emergence of a primordial hill, while those of Memphis identified their origins with the god Ptah, who created Egypt, its gods, and man through his heart and word. Carriers of power, the deities were represented by symbols of vital strength: a human body, an animal body, or a human body with animal head. Apis, the bull god of fertility, was associated with various gods: Ptah, Re, Osiris. Omnipresent goddess, Hathor wore horns on her head. Thus the ancient divinity symbols of Mureybet underlie the Egyptian religion.

Wonder brought the Egyptians to the discovery of the mystery of life, whose sacred value was represented by the *ankh* sign, which lived on through the millennia until Christianity. A new anthropology associating divine breath (*Ka*), personal conscience (*Ba*), and the immortal principle (*Akh*) to the body (*Zet*), led to the embalming of the deceased so as to assure them a happy immortality near the gods Re or Osiris.

Guardian of creation and life—a mission entrusted to him by the double crown identifying him as both Horus and Osiris—the Pharaoh was in charge of the construction of the temples, the houses of the gods where the priests, his delegates, ensured daily worship to the divine statues, so to maintain the order of the cosmos. The cosmos itself was entrusted to the goddess Maat, who granted universal truth, justice, and wisdom.

The Egyptian *homo religiosus* deeply influenced the thought of the Mediterranean peoples.

6. The ankh, from the hieroglyphic for life, is the most prevalent symbol in Egyptian art. Representing the gift of the gods, it was given to kings, placed under the nostrils of the dead so they could breath eternity, and inscribed everywhere. Here we see an ankh with Osiris, god of the dead, and the head of a jackal, symbol of desert life.

5. A map of Egypt (with East at the top) during the Old Kingdom. In boldface: the capitals with their dynasties. The territory unwinds along the course of the Nile, the impetuous challenge to the surrounding desert, giver of life with its beneficent muds and bringer of feared destruction with its floods. The great river that had been represented as a god of fertility, oriented the work of the ongoing peoples who lived nearby. The Old Kingdom inaugurated the era of the great pyramids. In the inset we see the map of the necropolis of Giza with the pyramids of Cheops, Chephren and Mycerinos. The pyramids were built inside burial complexes and expressed the desire to live on earth even after death.

5

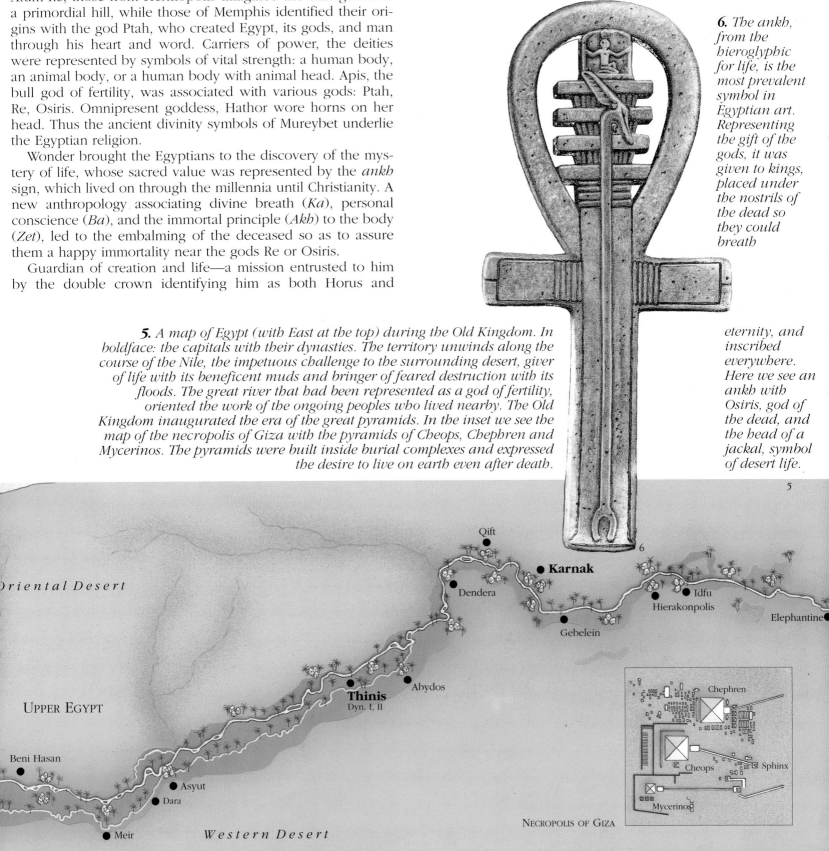

Qift

Karnak

Dendera

Idfu

Hierakonpolis

Elephantine

Oriental Desert

Gebelein

6

Abydos

Thinis
Dyn. I, II

UPPER EGYPT

Beni Hasan

Asyut

Dara

Meir

Western Desert

Chephren

Cheops

Sphinx

Mycerinos

NECROPOLIS OF GIZA

THE RELIGIOUS MAN IN THE GREAT CULTURE OF THE ORAL TRADITION

Very diverse in his expressions because of the numerous ethnic groups, the sub-Saharan African *homo religiosus* constitutes, however, a particular and specific type, shaped by a culture developed in the same mold. This culture carries the mark of the oral tradition: for it the word is first. Thus among the Dogons, after the creation of the cosmos by Amma, his son Nommo taught the word. The first word was a humid language, the second a luminous language, the third a musical spoken language. For the African man, the word is power, action, and meaning. Thanks to the Supreme Being, it has become the creator. Designated by various divine names, such as Bun (the sky), Niamian (firmament), Wuro, Nyambe, and Nzame, sometimes even nameless, this God is distant but paradoxically also very close to man. He is the guardian of the order of the world, of the harmony of beings, and of the meaning of existence.

The African man is convinced of the existence of two worlds, the visible one and the invisible one. Numerous are the myths that relate the separation of heaven and earth or that speak about the cosmos, in the center of which lies the sun-moon couple. In the invisible world reside the secondary gods, the spirits, and the civilizing geniuses, but also the ancestors, who remain linked to their descendants as guardian powers, assuring life, fertility, prosperity, but also reincarnation and traditions. Hence the importance of the seers, who are responsible for the initiation, for the transmission of messages from the ancestors, and for the ancestors' word as a vital source of energy. A true hierarchy of invisible powers watches over the family and people. Powers, ancestors, initiation, traditions of the past, messages from the invisible world, seers, and magicians weave the daily ties of the African *homo religiosus* with the invisible world, which is the world of the sacred and the real.

In daily living, the word is the creator and transmitter of the vital force coming from the invisible world. In this return to the origins, an important role is played by body positions, water, earth, air, fire, gestures, chants, cries, words, mimes, and colors—in short, the rich and complex ritual symbology of the feasts and daily life. Through the celebration of myths and the extreme diversity of the rites of initiation, purification, commemoration, propitiation, and thanksgiving, the African man

1. A mask representing a genius from Burkina Faso. The painted eyes refer to the capacity to perceive the invisible. In Africa, visual arts "speak," just like words.

consacrates birth, puberty, marriage, family, and death. He also gives a meaning to his own existence in an ordered cosmos. The solemnity and the splendor in the celebration of myths as well as the wealth and the emotional charge of the symbolic language during the ritual feasts contribute to making the African *homo religiosus*, immersed in an oral culture quite close to the cosmos, a precious model to better seize the impact of the symbol, the myth, and the rite in the formation of man's religious thought through the millennia.

3. The human body defines space, it differentiates it, and orients it. Thus the Dogon villages have a symbolic layout that organizes space in a human form. The head is the Council House, preceded to the north by the forge of the blacksmith, the primordial civilizing hero; to the sides, the hands of the village are the ritual houses of the women; at the center, the breast and womb are the houses of the families; and finally the feet are the common altars.

forge

HEAD · council house

houses of the families

BREAST

HANDS
ritual houses of the women

altars

FEET

3

2

2. A sculpted post used to hold up the roof of the Togu na, the Council House of the Dogon (Mali), seat of the "word" that governs communal life. The posts recall the ancestors who were the first to sit in a hut of the word. Here we see the imprint of the sandals of the Creator of the universe.

4

4. A harvest dance in Cameroon. The rhythms of nature are celebrated here by women, thus expressing through this ritual the ultimate bond between the fertility of the human body and the desired fruits of the earth.

8
THE SACRED DRAMA OF MAN'S RELIGIOUS ORIGIN

The peopling of Australia was started 40,000 years ago from Indonesia. Rock paintings and engravings, particularly numerous in Arnhem Land, are strewn across the territory, and mixed with more recent tree bark paintings, probably destined to initiation. The culture of the nowadays Aborigines is a lithic culture of Paleolithic hunters at the Aurignacian and Magdalenian level (meaning 22,000 years ago). The study of Aborigines' mythology has greatly contributed to drawing the face of the Australian *homo religiosus*.

At the end of a long debate between W. Schmidt, R. Pettazzoni, and M. Eliade, a belief in the Australian heavenly gods emerged. Baiame lives in heaven, he fertilizes the land, and the sun and moon are his messengers. It is the same for Daramulum, creator of the bull-roarer, an initiation instrument. Bundjil, the god of the Kulin Tribes, inhabits the highest heaven; he is the creator of earth, vegetation and man. Removed from the world, these gods signal their voice by thunder, lightning, wind, and the aurora borealis. Creators of mythical beings and men, they are also the revealers of mysteries such as the genealogies of tribes and the initiation rites.

For the Australian *homo religiosus*, the human Time started with the emergence of mythical ancestors who modified the contours and shapes of the landscapes and settled the tribe territories. This was the primordial Dreamtime, marked by the dynamism of life transmitted by active deities, who came to assure the fertility of the land and its populating by both men and animals, and to arrange sacred centers in space. The myths describe the Dreamtime as an era of creativity, emergence of mythical characters, behavior setting for men-women relations, and for family and social life. The myths about origins, ancestors, and work are like a mirror of society and religious life.

The initiation rites constitute an essential gear in the life of the human being and of the tribe. Created by the gods, sources of the sacred, these rites reenact events from the origins, are loaded with a symbology of death and resurrection, and lift the candidate from ignorance and the adolescent stage to a new birth, turning him into an adult person who is spiritual, fully conscious, knowing, and responsible to his tribe. In the course of the initiation the symbology of death by fire, the racket, the obscurity of the cave, and the dull and frightening sound of the bull-roarer are followed by the joy brought by the purification of the waters, the resurrection signs, the initiation to the stories of the tribe, the ritual dances, and the handing over of the *tjurunga*, a personal secret to keep.

The Australian *homo religiosus* believes in the afterlife of his superior soul, his "primordial and pre-existing spirit," who, after death, goes up to heaven with the help of a rope, an invisible tree, and the bright rays of the sun. In the abode of the ancestors it awaits reincarnation.

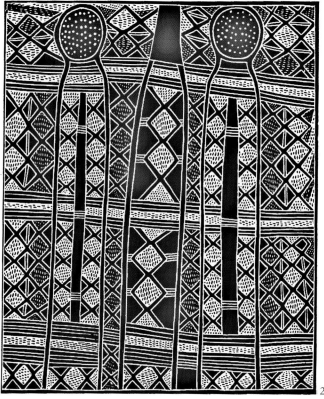

1. Eucalyptus bark. A specific type of eucalyptus (Eucalyptus tetradonta) provides the Australian aborigines from Arnhem Land and nearby islands with a base for exceptional paintings. The bark is removed from the treetrunk when it is still damp and elastic. It is then dried and flattened.
2. Art, even with its enormous local variations, always plays a central role in the Australian religious world. The intention of the bark paintings is instructional: it tells of mythic events in order to transmit their essence, and it is tied to other art forms like cave paintings, decorated objects, body painting and tattooing, music, dance, and narration; an indivisible whole that signals an untiring search for a link with the supernatural. Here we see the ancestor Wild Honey: the two central figures are trees, the diamonds are both the various elements of the beehive and the ancestor himself; the dots are the bees. The painting tells a story about places created by the ancestor and rites that celebrate his power.

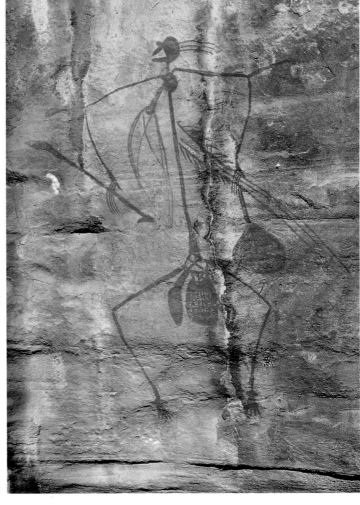

3. 4. 5. *An Australian bull-roarer. Tied to a rope, it is rotated on its axis, and then rapidly whirled in the air. It produces different sounds according to its speed and position. It is said that the bull-roarer is the voice of the Supreme Being, who created it.*
6. *According to the Aborigines, there are many spirits that take part in human happenings. Mimi are the ironic, astute and friendly ancestral spirits, who taught hunting, food gathering and painting. They are outlined in red pigment on rocks, whose crevices they inhabit. Here we see one Mimi spirit from Ubirr Rock in Kakadu National Park, Arnhem Land.*

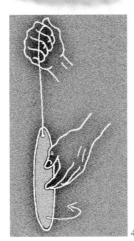

7. *Uluru (Ayers Rock) is a huge monolith in central Australia, surrounded by sacred caves rich with rock art. The Aborigines see the image of a mythic spirit in its shape.*

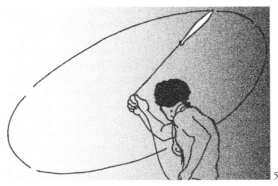

HOMO SYMBOLICUS, HOMO RELIGIOSUS

The preceding chapters bring us to see the symbols as primordial data for the conscience, the thought, the creativity and the life of the *homo religiosus*, according to the assessment of Mircea Eliade in his *Traité d'Histoire des Religions* (Paris, 1949). To the archaic man heaven directly revealed its transcendence, its strength, and its sacredness, because the symbol of the celestial vault was an agent of revelation. A vast network of symbols intervened in man's life and directed his religious conscience: among these cosmic symbols are the waters, the moon, the sun, the stars, the trees, and the mountains. The anthropological path of a constant exchange, at the imaginary level, between the human psyche and outside impulses, made man undergo a permanent growth and an always-new activity. His imagination allowed him to create signs and symbols of transcendency and of the divine, an extraordinary treasure for mankind's heritage.

Through the myths, man narrates events set at the origins, in the primordial and fabulous time of the beginnings, in order to explain existing realities. Thus the myth is a "sacred story" structured by means of symbology. Its repetition has an awakening function, it confers an experience of renewal to human action, and provides a model for daily behavior. For the religious man belonging to monotheisms that refer to historical founders—Jewish, Christian, Muslim—the place of the myths is taken by the sacred history, rooted in events and texts by the founders.

Rite is a part of the symbolic expression through which man looks for a vital contact with the transcendent reality, the divine, and God. The rite brings about a passage, or a transfer. The traces of numerous funeral rites from the Middle Paleolithic, the gestures of the worshippers in Valcamonica from the Neolithic, and the consecration rites at Sumer and in Egypt have been considered. The rite can allow the rebirth of a primordial event, it can be founding, or signify the communion with the divine: it is the case of the stretched arms of the worshippers.

Mircea Eliade wrote: "the symbolic thought is consubstantial to the human being." Through the symbol the cosmos speaks to man. The myth presents an exemplary model and exercises an exploratory function that aims at unveiling the link between man and the sacred. The rite exercises a mediatory function, it can initiate to a new birth or operate a sacralization. Symbol, myth, and rite, are essential for the activity of the religious man.

1

1. *A graphic representation of a statue called The Worshipper from Larsa, a Babylonian city south of the Euphrates. The joined hands placed at the height of the mouth and the bent knee of the individual from the ancient civilization of Mesopotamia embody a sense of dependence and prayer.*

4. *Generally, myths tell the story of creation, of how things came into existence. There are other myths that tell of the origins of peoples. Here we see an example from the pre-Columbian Boturini Codex: a population leaves its homeland and meets a god in a cave. The eight tribes, behind their chiefs, erect a temple to the god but a bad omen, the broken tree, will bring tears. The Aztec Tribe, under advice from the god, will break away, guided by new omens. Thus an establishing event is tied to superior forces.*

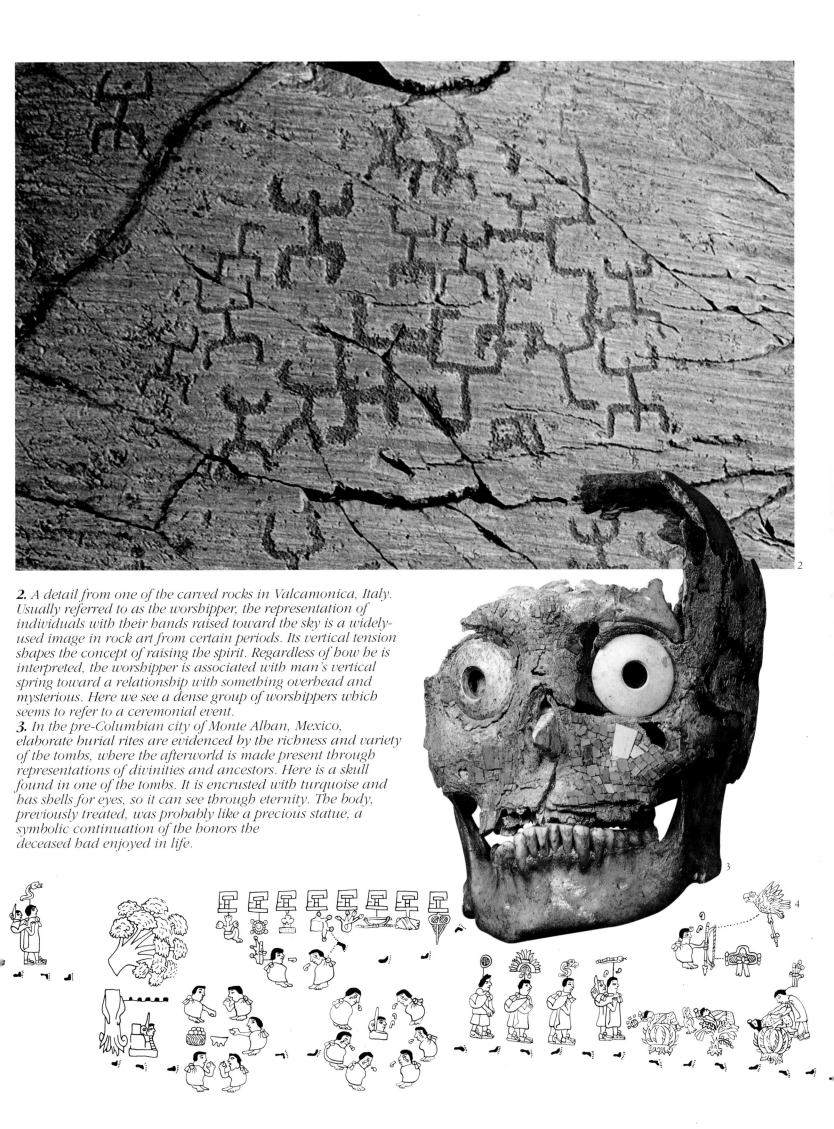

2. *A detail from one of the carved rocks in Valcamonica, Italy. Usually referred to as the worshipper, the representation of individuals with their hands raised toward the sky is a widely-used image in rock art from certain periods. Its vertical tension shapes the concept of raising the spirit. Regardless of how he is interpreted, the worshipper is associated with man's vertical spring toward a relationship with something overhead and mysterious. Here we see a dense group of worshippers which seems to refer to a ceremonial event.*

3. *In the pre-Columbian city of Monte Alban, Mexico, elaborate burial rites are evidenced by the richness and variety of the tombs, where the afterworld is made present through representations of divinities and ancestors. Here is a skull found in one of the tombs. It is encrusted with turquoise and has shells for eyes, so it can see through eternity. The body, previously treated, was probably like a precious statue, a symbolic continuation of the honors the deceased had enjoyed in life.*

THE RELIGIOUS MAN AND THE UNIVERSAL EXPERIENCE OF THE SACRED

The religious man of the great civilizations has created the vocabulary of the sacred so as to give an account of a specific experience of which he declares himself the witness: the experience of his link with the Mystery of the Invisible, and with the Divine which determines his behavior. The religious anthropology studies the religious man as a creator and user of the symbolic ensemble of the sacred and as a carrier of religious beliefs that direct his life and behavior. Each religion has its specific position regarding man, the human condition, the integration of man in the world and society. All this influences the religious man.

In India there is no sacred without the divine: the sacred is a manifestation of the divine and a mediatory element between it and man. The Indian religious man considers the divine as eternally pure and totally distinct from the world. An active force, it manifests through phenomena, beings, things, and people who are called *punya*, a word that expresses the radiance of sanctity. Furthermore, sacred symbolic expression in India is very rich: gestures, colors, rites, temples, liturgies, and processions.

In Israel the episode of the burning Bush and the Sinai Alliance show that Yahwe, the holy God par excellence, one and creator, intervened in the history of His people and established

1. Rapa Nui, or Easter Island. The rainbow has always evoked in men the image of a bridge leading to the sky, in a spiritual travel to reach the divine. 2. A graphic rendition of a fresco from an Egyptian tomb in Thebes. The tree, symbol of the relationship between earth and heaven, nourishes the Pharaoh. 3. A billabong, the Australian word for a pool of water found in a dry river bend. Covered by water lilies, the billabong is the habitat for water birds and, like any environmental element, a trace of mythic times, even more so because of the role water plays: fertility opposing the desert.

Himself against all the idols of the Canaanite cults. He demanded a worship complying to his sanctity and rejected all the former bloody cults. In the Koran, Allah is the source of the sacred because he is the unique holy God. The Muslim totally submits to god and considers the Koran as the Sacred Book par excellence. For him, the *baraka* is the benediction of Allah and is linked to his sanctity. Islam has its sacred times and spaces, which are important in order to live the religious experience of the faithful and of the community of the Prophet.

The experience of the *homo christianus* is original and unique in the world of religions because it is based on the mystery of God the Father, Son, and Spirit, and on Jesus Christ the Messiah, Son incarnate who completes the creation and becomes a New Adam in the economy of salvation that he inaugurates. The experience of the sacred continuously resorts to the biblical, cosmic, and anthropological symbolism in order to develop the doctrines of the New Testament and those of the Fathers of the Church on the mission of Jesus Christ and the Holy Spirit. The experience of the Christian sacred is lived on four levels: first, Jesus Christ the mediator; second, the sacred of the sacramental signs; third, the pedagogical sacred; and fourth, the daily sanctification.

4. A monk bent over the pages of a prayer book in the Monastery of Karsha, Zanskar Valley (India).
5. An Islamic groom prays before his wedding in Sikkim, India.
6. On the feast of the Assumption, the statue of the Virgin is carried in procession: it is one of the most popular forms of Catholic devotion. Calasca, Italy.

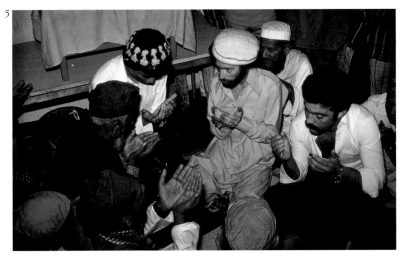

7. 8. Behind the Jewish boy, absorbed in the scrolls of the law, is the picture of a fire, which is the memory of the theophany (the visible manifestation of God to mankind) of the burning Bush and a symbol of renewal. 9. A Tibetan altar consecrated to the mountain gods, whom the people of the area tie to the family and the clan. Annual rites are held to restore the prayer stones, arrows, and flags.

GLOSSARY

Acheulian: term used to designate the industry of bifacial tools at Saint-Acheul near Amiens, then spread to all bifacial tools of the European Lower Paleolithic (France, Spain, Italy, England) and also to those of Olduvai in Africa.

Aurignacian: first cultural stage of the Upper Paleolithic. It started toward 36,000 years ago (after the Mousterian); during this period the first European artists appeared, using burins, producing cupules and pierced sticks, engraving stone, and leaving numerous burials. It is the culture of the Cro-Magnon and Grimaldi Men, a classical type of *Homo sapiens sapiens* at his beginnings.

Australopithecs: group of fossil Hominidae whose first representative was discovered in South Africa in 1925. Today they are known due to numerous remains, found in sub-Saharan Africa from Ethiopia to South Africa. They cover a period from 4 million to 1 million years ago. They are small size bipeds (1 meter to 1.5 meter), and are closer to man than to apes.

Baraka: Arab word meaning the blessing that assures prosperity. Islam has tied *baraka* to places, personages, mosques, and places of pilgrimage. It is a notion previous to Islam and coming from the vocabulary of the nomads: prosperity, fertility, success, herd growth, and abundance of vegetation. In Islam, *baraka* is the blessing of Allah, a divine prerogative.

Consecration (rites of): the word derives from the latin *cum* (with) and *sacrum* (sacred). It indicates the practice, spread throughout the most diverse cultures, to bestow upon specific realities a particular religious value. Such practice includes gestures and ceremonies that exalt the sacred meaning of places and images and that can also grant divine authority to a human being.

Cupule: (from the latin *cupula*). The scholars of prehistory give this name to a little cup dug into stone or rock with a tool. These cupules appear in little groups and are held to be the sign of a ritual offering to a deity. The faithful maybe poured a liquid offering into them.

Dogon: tribe from Mali, residing by the south-west bend of the Niger river, in a mountainous region called the "cliffs of Bandiagara," where the rainy season lasts only four months a year.

Eucologe: liturgical Byzantine book containing the celebrant's prayers of the Eucharist liturgy, the divine office, the ritual for sacraments, blessings, and consecrations. In the Latin Church it corresponds to the liturgical book called Sacramentary.

Heliopolis: Egyptian city of the Old Kingdom, famous for the worship of the solar god Atum-Re. At the beginning of the third dynasty King Djeser centralized this worship under his authority by associating the clergy to his government. Afterwards, Heliopolis became the center of a solar theology focused on the creator god Re. Nowadays the city has disappeared.

Hermopolis: city of Middle Egypt, 300 km south of Cairo. Today some ruins are all that is left of it. Under the Old Kingdom it was famous for its theology, centered on the god Thot, who was the judge par excellence, the god of laws and the creator of institutions.

Hominization: ensemble of the physical, physiological, and mental evolutive processes that mark the passage from primates to humans.

Homo erectus: discovered at Java in 1891 (*Pithecanthropus*), he was also found after 1960 to the east of Lake Turkana, Africa, where he lived 1.5 million years ago. His cranial capacity increased from 800 to 1,250 cm^3. He occupied a progressively large part of the Ancient World: southeast Asia, China, Africa, and southern Europe, and disappeared about 150,000 years ago. He mainly refined the lithic industry and invented fire (Zhoukoudian near Peking and Terra Amata, on the slope of Mount Boron, near Nice). He marked a great progress: big game hunting, food cooking, sheds as habitats, tools and weapons, and language.

Homo habilis: the oldest representative of *Homo* genus actually known. He was discovered at Olduvai in Tanzania, at Koobi Fora to the east of Lake Turkana in Kenya, and in South Africa. He lived more than 2 million years ago and created the first culture, called Oldowan, characterized by stone artifacts: choppers and bifaces. Living as a hunter-gatherer, he shaped his habitat. In evolution, he represents quite a qualitative jump.

homo religiosus: we leave phylogenesis to enter anthropology. Created by religious history scholars, this expression designates man as the subject of the experience of the sacred.

Homo sapiens: a descendant of *Homo erectus*, he is characterized by his cranial capacity up to 1,400 cm^3. His first representatives date back to 300,000 years ago. In Europe, he is represented by a particular type: the Neanderthal Man, who lived between 80,000 and 35,000 years ago. With *Homo sapiens* the first burials appear: Qafzeh and Skhul in Israel, dating back to 90,000 years ago, and associated with a Mousterian culture.

Homo sapiens sapiens: man of the Upper Paleolithic who probably came from Africa and derived from *Homo sapiens*. He spread throughout Europe from 40,000 years ago, and reached further in the Ancient and New World, undergoing an adaptive diversification owing to the geographical and climatic differences. An ancestor of the modern man, he created cave art, multiplied the tombs and the burial rites, lived as a hunter-gatherer, invented the bow, and led a well organized social life. The funerary ritual and the furniture art know a great development.

homo symbolicus: connotation by which the anthropologists designate a faculty specific to man, expressed through his cultural creativity, and seen as a result of his imagination, thanks to which man is capable of perceiving the invisible from the visible.

Ideogram: minimal graphic sign constituting, in certain writing forms, an element giving a basic sense. It is the case of Chinese writing, for example.

Initiation: the term indicates a set of rites and teachings whose intent is to produce a radical transformation of the religious and social status of the initiated. Such rites and teachings, besides fully introducing the candidate into a society and into its cultural and religious values, symbolize the relation between death and rebirth, where "death" indicates the end of an existence with no true culture, and "rebirth," or resurrection, signals the passage to a new life.

Magdalenian: a prestigious culture from the end of the Upper Paleolithic. It takes its name from La Madeleine (Dordogne). Assegai, bone harpoons, lithic tools, painted caves, furniture art, and the caves of Lascaux, Rouffignac, Font-de-Gaume, Chancelade in France, and Altamira in Spain. The Magdalenian cave and furniture art reached its peak between 20,000 and 12,000 years ago.

Memphis: toward 3,000 B.C. at the entrance of the Nile Delta, near a temple of the god Ptah, the king Menes built the fort of the White Wall, which became the capital of the two Egypts: it is Mennofer, called Memphis by the Greeks, and of which some ruins remain.

Mousterian: term used by G. de Mortillet from 1869 to designate the industry of Le Moustier (Dordogne), which was characterized by points, single face scrapers and by very flat bifaces. Later an important classification was introduced in order to specify the regional features of this main culture of the Middle Paleolithic, which eventually spread throughout all Europe, especially due to the Neanderthal Man.

Myth: story relating events of the origins, and destined to be a behavior model for life. The myth is a sacred story, symbolic and exemplary for the life of men and people.

Mythogram: representation system characteristic of the Upper Paleolithic art. Without a narrative line, it needed the reciting of oral myth, whose elements we have lost. According to Leroi-Gourhan, the mythograms are the essential structure of cave art.

Natufian: a civilization between gathering and agriculture. Its denomination comes from Wadi en Natuf in Western Judea. It existed from 10,000 to 8,300 B.C. It started with man leaving rock shelters, and continued with the settlement of the populations of the Near East, who kept on living from gathering. Villages were created, artifacts were developed, but agriculture was not yet born.

Neolithic: in the 8th millennium a great transformation took place in the Near East: the domestication of plant and animal species, the birth of agriculture, and the introduction of the production economy. To this transformation corresponds an ideological and psychological transformation: creation of the first representations of the divinity and modification in the conception of the sacred (J. Cauvin).

Olduvai: one of the main sites of East Africa, between the Rift Valley and Tanzania. It is a 50 km long and 90 m high gorge. Fossil records revealed the origins of *Homo habilis* and of the first culture: the Oldowan, dating to more than 2 million years ago. We are probably at the origins of humanity.

Paleolithic: term created in 1865 by John Lubbock to designate the Ancient Stone Age, cut but not polished, and to distinguish it from the New Stone Age, which was characterized by the polishing of the axes. The Paleolithic starts with the first culture and thus covers more than 2 million years of prehistory. The distinction of three periods in this rich and complex time is based upon chronological, archeological, cultural, and paleoanthropological criteria. The LOWER PALEOLITHIC is the work of *Homo habilis* and of *Homo erectus*. The MIDDLE PALEOLITHIC, which spreads from 200,000 to 35,000 years ago, is the work of *Homo sapiens neanderthalensis*. His successor, *Homo sapiens sapiens,* created the UPPER PALEOLITHIC, which around 10,000 B.C. made place for a new culture called Mesolithic, a transition toward the Neolithic.

Phylogenesis: formation mode of the species and their development during evolution.

Punya: a sacred term in India applied to water, an estate, a temple purified by rites, a place of pilgrimage, a tradition, to beings who live in sanctity, and to texts. *Punya* is opposed to wrong and evil. It is also a force through which the divine acts.

Sacred: the term *sakros* comes from an archaic inscription found on a stone in the Roman Forum. It brings us to the origins of the sacred in Rome and in the Indo-European world, where the radical *sak-* has given birth to the verb *sancire*, meaning "to confer validity, reality." *Sak-* is thus at the foundation of the real. This notion is at the same time juridical, metaphysical, and religious. The experience of the sacred implies the discovery of an absolute reality that humans perceive as transcendental.

Shamanism: socio-religious phenomenon coming from some Toungouse ethnic groups of Siberia, where it designated the action of an individual capable of entering in contact with the supernatural world in order to help the community to face the daily difficulties. It is related with ecstasy, magic, religion, possession, hunting religion, fire mastery, and magic flight. Enlarged forms of Shamanism can be found in China, Japan, and the Hungarian world.

Sumerian: the country of the Sumerians, in the most southern part of Mesopotamia, was enclosed between the Tigris and Euphrates rivers, in a region fertilized by the canals, dug by man. Coming from a still unknown land, the Sumerians introduced, around 3,300 B.C., writing, cylinder-seals, architecture, and built the first big city-states: Uruk, Ur, Eridu, Lagash, and Shurupak. The keystone of their sacred culture was called **me**, which were a set of rules of universal and unchanging limits observed by both gods and men.

Tjurunga: these engraved wood or stone tablets are the secret signs of initiation in the Aboriginal tribes. The *tjurunga* are kept in sacred and secret places to which the neophytes are taken during the initiation ceremony. Each one receives his *tjurunga* tablet; the old people explain the inscriptions and the ornaments that cover it. The initiated will watch over it as a personal and precious possession, because it opens him the way of the secrets of life and of gods.

INDEX